Arcane Fraternal Orders

By

Eric F. Magnuson

Fimbul Winter Books

Arcane Fraternal Orders

ISBN-13: 978-1477459492

ISBN-10: 1477459499

Arcane Fraternal Orders

Fimbul Winter Trilogy III

Attainment for two magickal
orders based upon Evolutionary
Libertarian principles. Elucidates
revolution magick by creating a
mindset conducive to establishing
world liberty and peace via
democratic means.

To

Ralph M. Lewis

Contents

Introductory Note

This essay below is found elsewhere and is offered again here as an introduction. The impatient reader may wonder what any of this has to do with revolution. Please keep reading. There is much of value to be learned here.

Magick and Revolution

Magick is the carefully directed use of make-believe, among other things, to the end of securing conditions greatly desired.

The use of magickal procedures is best confined to ceremonies honoring important ideals and events, or for the celebration of the seasons. It is usually best to achieve specific goals in life without the use of ritual procedures of any kind unless absolutely necessary. The ethical problems involved in trying to exert influence over other people at a distance are complex and parallel the issues surrounding the use of subliminal messages and surveillance.

Having reconciled beforehand the moral rightness of any working, the actualization of desired change in the external world can be effected within the context of magickal procedures thusly:

1. By ordinary, mundane methods, including all those known to profane science.

2. Through the manipulation of ancient archetypal imagery to inspire one's own subconscious mind to bring about the desired result. The latter day term for watered-down versions of this is "psychodrama."

3. By inspiring the subconscious minds of others, either present or at a physical distance through telepathy, or in the future, utilizing their expected clairvoyant reaction to things enacted now.

4. Directly, at a distance, by telekinesis.

5. By any combination of the above, including total astral projection.

6. By other methods utilized by certain individuals, not necessarily understood even by them, which "might" be working anyway, even accidentally. These also in combination with any other methods.

7. By necromantic processes, which the author must urgently warn against. Case histories abound.

Revolution Magick in this context is simply any or all of the above applied to the goal of massive societal change. Nordic kinsmen find "Ritual für den Tod" on the Internet.

Attainment within Arcane Orders

Evolutionary dualism is explained in the book "Evolutionary Psychology". There are two arcane orders based upon this principle. The systems of attainment for each are designed to speed up personal growth, by first enhancing recognition of what actually constitutes growth. Both systems and a very strange section "The Inner Chamber" are described on the following pages.

Progression to a higher grade in either order must celebrate only a major event, lesson learned, or advance in personal development, and must correspond to the traditional characteristics of the particular deity attributed for that grade. Sometimes attainment may not be identified until much later in life. Many of the grades may actually have been attained long before entering the particular order.

Absolute honesty and self-knowledge are required to progress properly here. Inner satisfaction comes not from recognition by others, but from oneness with the higher self. The Order of the Ten Rayed Star and the Order of Yggdrasil should prove of interest in this regard.

Order of the Ten Rayed Star

Ne~ 1 TRS

November 22, 1996
The Witch House
Lake Wildwood, California

The Ten Rayed Star

The Ten Rayed Star is a Pentacle and a very pure representation of evolutionary dualism. It is the two traditional Pentagrams interlaced and has it's own planetary and elemental attributions (22). Starting with the uppermost point, the planets are represented at each point thusly moving deosil: Sun, Saturn, Venus, Neptune, Mercury, Moon, Jupiter, Mars, Uranus, Pluto.

The Ten Rayed Star is also an arcane order. Each point represents a separate component order. The specific purpose of each is shown in the chart below. Only complete attainment of eleven degrees in a component order constitutes one degree of attainment in the Ten Rayed Star. Appropriate modifications should be made here to suit the mythological heritage of the practitioner: pantheon, component order, and grade names.

The TRS is open to all 8th Degree initiates of the Order of Yggdrasil. Entry is by self-initiation or within autonomous local groups. There is no fee. Before undertaking TRS activity the aspirant should write and retain an essay about past activities and future objectives in this entire context. New insights should be appended at intervals. Attainment here takes a great deal of time and is not for the impatient (23).

The component orders OM, CW, OS, and OR are merely systems for reckoning various types of personal growth. Although they have been in use for many years and technically have membership, they are not useful for group activity.

Eric Fenris Magnuson

Ten Rayed Star

SolSys	Character	Norse	Grade	Component Order	Purpose
Future	Destiny	Yggdrasi	11	Council of Asgard aft Ragnarok	Life's Highest Purposes
Pluto	Transformation	Hel	10	Order of Yggdrasi in the East	Libertarian Revolution
Neptune	Mysticism	Mimir	9	Order of the Runemasters	Intuition and Wisdom
Uranus	Change	Odin	8	The WLO	Worldwide Education
Saturn	Perfection	Fenris	7	Order of the White Wolf(24)	Special Achievement
Jupiter	Justice	Thor	6	Sentinels of Thor	Judicial Equilibrium
Mars	Might	Tyr	5	Legion of Ragnarok	Martial Prowess
Sun	Power	Balder	4	Order of Suna	Integrated Higher Self
Venus	Passion	Freya	3	Coven of the Witches(25)	Sex and Romance
Mercury	Magick	Kvasir	2	Children of Odin	Archetypal Magick
Moon	Energy	Garm	1	Order of Yggdrasi in the North	Spiritual Energizing
Earth	Stability	Frigga	0	Order of Midgard	Status and Schedule

The Grades

Component Order	Norse Designation	Grade	Norse	Traditional Latin
Council of Asgard after Ragnarok	White Wizard	11	Yggdrasi	Ipsissimus
Order of Yggdrasi in the East	Raven Friend	10	Hel	Reditor in Vitam
Order of the Runemasters	Runemaster	9	Mimir	Illuminatus
The WLO	Gray Wizard	8	Odin	Magus
Order of the White Wolf	Warrior of Light	7	Fenris	Adeptus Exemplus
Sentinels of Thor	Ally of the Norns	6	Thor	Adeptus Exemptus
Legion of Ragnarok	Berserker	5	Tyr	Adeptus Bello
Order of Suna	Dragonmaster	4	Balder	Adeptus Pace
Coven of the Witches	Witch Friend	3	Freya	Voluptarius
Children of Odin	Norse Magician	2	Kvasir	Philosophus
Order of Yggdrasi in the North	Seeker of Thule	1	Garm	Practicus
Order of Midgard	Oathmaker	0	Frigga	Zelator
Preliminary Attainment	Viking Kinsman	Atria		Neophyte

The Work

Grade	Norse	Activity
11	White Wizard	Total commitment to refinements after the main necessary work is done
10	Raven Friend	Total commitment to the necessary work ahead
9	Runemaster	Shedding off of all distraction. Development of intuitive inner certainty
8	Gray Wizard	Application of all knowledge and most energy to productive Libertarian change
7	Warrior of Light	Honing of special natural talents or interests to higher degrees of prowess
6	Ally of the Norns	Development of clear perceptions regarding justice tempered with compassion
5	Berserker	Channeling of righteous anger into disciplined martial attainment to be used later
4	Dragonmaster	Study of the World. Recognition of what is needed. Proper balance of activity
3	Witch Friend	Learning of humility and synergy in sexual and romantic relationships
2	Norse Magician	Discovery and practice of one's own true spiritual heritage
1	Seeker of Thule	Period of diligent study and contemplation. Eclectic free thought
0	Oathmaker	Workbook for recognition of progress and for designating work to be done
Atria	Viking Kinsman	Carry over from previous lifetimes leading to the Quest

Footnotes:

22. See Scroll E in "Traditional Arcane Teachings" by Eric F. Magnuson.

23. The author for example, has no expectation of full attainment within current lifetime.

24. Not to be confused with other orders of the same name.

25. For women this can be Coven of the Warlocks. Can be an after-the-fact or forward looking hypothetical harem of the heart. It can also be rewarding here to systematize other basic pleasures.

TRS Order Foundings

Liber Eventorum

February 12, 1883	Burial Hill Plymouth MA: World Libertarian Order Order of Yggdrasil in the North (1)
Autumn Sabbat 1985	Surry Lake NH: Special Orders for Valor WLO Werewolves
Spring Sabbat 1993	Echo Lake NH: Children of Odin Order of the White Wolf (2)
Plow Charming 1997	Pyramid Lake NV: Order of Midgard
May Day 2003	MGM Dome NV: Coven of the Witches
Midsummer 2014	Great Salt Lake UT: Order of Suna
Freyfaxi 2014	Mt Hood OR: Legion of Ragnarok
Autumn Sabbat 2014	Glacier Park WY: Sentinels of Thor
Samhain 2014	Crater Lake OR: Order of Ten Rayed Star
Yule Sabbat 2014	Stonehenge WA: Order of the Runemasters
Liberty Day 2015	Mt Lassen CA: Order of Yggdrasil in the East
Spring Sabbat	*Mt Baker WA: Order of Asgard after Ragnarok*

Salem Willows

Burial Hill

Surry Lake

Echo Lake

Pyramid Lake

MGM Grand Hotel

Stansbury Bay

Mount Hood

Glacier National Park

Crater Lake

America's Stonehenge

Mt. Lassen

Footnotes:

1. One can progress further. The Order of Yggdrasil is open to Libertarians of the 9th degree in any system effectively comprehending the principles of evolutionary dualism, even if terminology differs.

2. Not to be confused with other orders of the same name

The Order of Yggdrassil

"Do what thou wilt shall be the whole of the Law"

~ Aleister Crowley ~

Herein we find esoteric adventure for Libertarian activists - Revolution Magick. Although there is no affiliation with indigenous kindreds or spirituality in this context, we use an Old Norse symbol as our inspiration. The World Tree is a fine universal representation of steadfastness and eternal life through evolution. We find its counterpart in many other cultures.

The Order of Yggdrasil is a chivalrous order of knighthood for men and women who possess the courage to love, and the integrity to live, morally in accordance with evolutionary principals. The basic ideals will be readily comprehended by all true Libertarians. The esoteric and mystical principles employed however, will only be understood by those of the 9th degree in arcane orders effectively comprehending the principles of evolutionary dualism, even if terminology for this differs. Membership is therefore proposed only for initiates at this appropriate level of attainment.

The next section "The Inner Chamber" is actually a short self-contained book. It creates a frame of mind conducive to establishing world Libertarianism by democratic means. It does this inspirationally by depicting a daydream which prefigures a time when the revolution will necessarily have progressed much further than at the time of writing. It is a very complete system with bylaws and rituals. There are descriptions of flags, ceremonial armor, dress and field uniforms, and decorations for valor. Symbols are eclectic, very traditional, and from ancient mythology. All of this, of course, involves a much higher level of activism than we hope will ever become necessary.

Grades within the Order of Yggdrasil

Degrees of Attainment

Appropriate pantheon reflecting practitioner's heritage should be attributed here. "The Work" for each grade is essentially the same within any component order as for the Ten Rayed Star as a whole. The difference is simply one of focus, reflecting the specific purpose of the component order. In the OY the activity for each grade attainment is dedicated to World Libertarian Revolution.

Solar Sys	Character	Pantheon	Grade	Attainment	Traditional Grade
Future (1)	Destiny		11		Ipsissimus
Pluto	Transformation		10		Reditor in Vitam
Neptune	Mysticism		9		Illuminatus
Uranus	Change		8		Magus
Saturn	Perfection		7		Adeptus Exemplus
Jupiter	Justice		6		Adeptus Exemptus
Mars	Might		5		Adeptus Bello
Sun	Power		4		Adeptus Pace
Venus	Passion		3		Voluptarius
Mercury	Magick		2		Philosophus
Moon	Energy		1		Practicus
Earth	Stability		0		Zelator
			Atria		Neophyte

Footnote: 1. Future evolution on Earth

The Greatest of All Quests

"Unthinking individuals will make synonymous things that are not. Country, government, and 'the people' are not the same thing. Country is a geographically defined area within which exists the potential for absolute individual liberty. Government is that group of subverted collectivist manipulators in the service of international finance who prevent this liberty from occurring. The 'people' are that majority of naive and severely deluded individuals who aid and abet government in doing this."

"When an enemy and it's aims are clearly defined, a war against such enemy can be fought and won by individuals and small groups unknown to each other, and without any central organized coordination of activity. Individual clandestine activity actually confers the advantage since it makes mass retaliation impossible, and completely eliminates any capacity for infiltration. There must however, be a strong spiritual unity based on clearly defined goals and principles."

The Order of Yggdrasil is open only to those who have attained 9th degree in any spiritual system effectively comprehending the principles of evolutionary dualism. Differences in terminology for this are unimportant (1).

The Quest is that the evolutionary expression of all life forms on Earth be allowed to flourish unimpeded. The task consists in eliminating, through education, of all devolutionary forces on Earth. This means worldwide actualization of what we conceptualize as a World Libertarian Order currently lying dormant everywhere. The inevitable attainment of this ideal is here symbolized as humanity finally standing up totally free in the bright pure Light of Day. This concept is refereed to poetically as "Aethemera" (2).

This is not to suggest that someday there should be one country or even a confederation of countries. Separate sovereign Libertarian republics can be less easily subverted back to collectivism than one nation. This, instead, should simply be thought of as a symbolic principle underlying Libertarian action, as the higher potential initially for one's own country.

The Quest then is the establishment of a World Libertarian Order consisting of separate Libertarian republics, not all at once but eventually, time frames here being determined by the degree of understanding and will to Liberty of individual peoples throughout the world.

The Quest is the longest and grimmest that can be undertaken. It requires unlimited personal strength, a completely unfailing and uncompromising will, plus a tremendous spiritual courage in the face of always overwhelming odds.

Formal entry into the Order of Yggdrasil requires total commitment to the principles of absolute individual Liberty. Self-initiation is performed in the field, this being augmented by an in absentia ceremony performed at headquarters.

Such should not be entered into hurriedly or for selfish reasons. There is no room in any of this for personal obstacles of a lower nature. Absolute self-mastery is necessary and must be achieved as a prerequisite to effective knighthood. There will be pleasure and glory enough of the kind that matters when mankind is well on the way to finally standing in the clear Light of Day.

Hail Yggdrasil!

Eric Fenris Magnuson
10:04 AM, July 2, 1983
Ravenhurst in the mountains
During a lightning storm and downpour

What follows shows much about the early years.

Introduction

to the

Order of Yggdrasil

Dirk A. Lokison (3)

10 OYN

Freyfaxi 1983
Boston

Liber Aethemerae" (4) is the text of the original document read by Sir Fenris of Ravenhurst (5) putting forth the heroic concept of Aethemera at the founding ceremony on Burial Hill in Plymouth, Massachusetts on February 12, 1983. It is refered to, but not reproduced, here.

"Liber Sangrealis" is the original text founding the WLO and the Order of Yggdrasil (6). This outlines to some extent, methods to be used in the accomplishment of the Quest. It is required however, that original creative genius be diligently applied in this area in accordance with one's own abilities and courage. Names appearing originally as signatures, were "consigned to flame" as part of the ceremony and have been omitted from this text for reasons of personal privacy.

"Liber Fides" constitutes the Bylaws of the Order.

"Liber Heraldicae," in keeping with ancient tradition, has given us colors and arms for the Order.

It is appropriate that the Oath of Knighthood be taken as Part V of "Ritualis Grandis Initiatii" on the morning of the first

Sabbat subsequent to the qualified initiate's decision to enter the Order (7). An even better time, if it causes little delay, is on the morning of Founding Day (8) with the Oath immediately following Part IV of "Commemoration" which is performed at Solar Noon every February 12.

Also here is "Liber Historiae Occasi," a chart which chronicles certain events, some undoubtedly mythical, most verifiable, and all of special interest to initiates.

"Liber Eventorum" is a list of the very recent main events connected with the founding of the Order and Magnuson's defining of the Quest.

Dirk the Sun Warrior ~

Having sojourned recently in the vicinity of the Nile

———

Membership in the Order of Yggdrasil:

Exactly as in the WLO, members are encouraged to act creatively. It must be stressed that there is never physical contact between headquarters and members in the field, nor are we seeking any dialogue or pen-pal relationship with members. We are lone-wolf Libertarians, not fraternizers. Individuals can be united in action, even without specific knowledge of each other, if they are first united in spirit.

Members desiring social fellowship are authorized to create their own chapters locally and to recruit others. New members are required to pay life membership. All members or subgroups act autonomously and all activities must be in keeping with the principals of Evolutionary Libertarianism outlined in the book "World Libertarian Revolution" mentioned herein.

Footnotes:

1. Explained in "Evolutionary Psychology" by the current author. Until people become truly free within themselves, there will be little impetus to change society. The personal liberation of large numbers of people on an individual basis is a necessary prerequisite to world Libertarianism, because only a consensus majority of free thinking individuals will rise to effect the emancipation of entire countries.

2. From the Greek: Aether, meaning Light; and Hemera, meaning Day. Members of Nordic ancestry may prefer the Swedish word for this, which is "Dagsljus."

3. He, his wife, and parents were murdered in Canada by radical Socialists in 1985. See "The Adventures of Eric F. Magnuson".

4. "A Further Declaration of Independence" is within the OY, known as Liber Aethemerae.

5. Eric Fenris Magnuson. Knights are called "Sir" or "Lady" because of traditional values connected with chivalry. This is not to suggest any secular rank among the peerage of Europe.

6. In essence, the OY should be thought of as simply the esoteric appendage of the WLO.

6. Material from here forward will be most easily comprehended by those familiar with "Traditional Arcane Teachings" by E. F. Magnuson, wherein are outlined many things, including useful ritual procedures.

8. Will be called Liberty Day among the general population.

Liber Sangrealis (12)

Ne~ 8 OYN

February 2, 1983
Ravenhurst
Royalston, Massachusetts

"Further, let it be Proclaimed among the Wise

This day of February 12, 1983

That all Knights and Ladies here signing have organized
themselves into a purposeful body, now formed as:

The Order of Yggdrasil

the esoteric inner circle of
The World Libertarion Order

Both deriving their just and rightful authority through the members
by: their careful observation of the continuing lessons of history,
their profound understanding and mastery of the great Liber
Mundi, their arduous study and initiation into the Ancient Mysteries
and their direct and absolute knowledge of Universal Will. The
World Tree Yggdrasil herein symbolizes an unimpeded future for
the Evolutionary Expression of all living things.

Towards fulfillment of the purpose of this Order, it's Knights do,
in the Great Name of Yggdrasil, pledge themselves:

(The Names)

To perpetually strive towards undefiled wisdom and to continually
bring to the attention of their fellow Knights and Ladies any and all
information which could reasonably be construed as having the
potential for increasing individual Liberty, Earthly happiness, or
personal spiritual development.

To, among the profane, dedicate themselves to the promoting of knowledge, truth, and Light through the initiation of such action as will reflect a careful consideration of the relative development of the individuals in question.

To give their lives and arms in service to the Quest, Liberty Triumphant and Eternal, in unfailing vigilance under Sun and Moon and Stars to the end of days.

Love is the Law. Love Under Will.

Hail Yggdrasil! "

———

Bylaws of The Order of Yggdrasil

Liber Fides

All but one of the original bylaws of the Order of Yggdrasil were written in a way which pertained only to a small group of warrior-magicians and their ladies, all known to each other and meeting on the mornings of sabbat days prior to the rituals and festivities at various places of pilgrimage throughout the world.

As the Order is now constituted, all but one of the original bylaws have become irrelevant and have been amended. That one original bylaw appears first below while those that follow are of slightly more recent origin and together constitute a skeleton of current operating procedure to be used by knights throughout the world. The Oath of Allegiance appears at the end of this section.

Eric F. Magnuson

February 11, 1990
Castle on the Green
Lyndonville, Vermont

The Bylaws:

1. Standards and arms of the Order are in existence and are described elsewhere. Eric Fenris Magnuson is founder and Grandmaster of the Order and will appoint his successor. The duties of Grandmaster involve only the dissemination of material designed to educate the individual and to sustain a spiritual unity animating leaderless resistance to collectivist tyranny.

2. It is understood that the principles of the Order are outlined at length in the book known as "World Libertarian Revolution" by Eric Fenris Magnuson and that after diligent study of this material the candidate will, for purpose of self-examination, write an essay summarizing the problems which have beset the continuing Evolutionary Expression of life on Earth and what can be done in his own case to help solve these problems. The candidate should keep this essay and append new material as he grows in understanding.

3. All members of the Order of Yggdrasil should think of themselves as Libertarian in terms of political ideology but as considerably more activist than usual in terms of creative methodology for the implementation of Libertarian solutions.

4. Individual Knights or groups of Knights are to be completely autonomous and are empowered to self-initiate as herein described and to act creatively in establishing procedure for the conduct of meetings and of all activities pertaining to the Quest, so long as all such activities are in all ways totally consistent with the principles of the Order (13).

5. It is expected of the individual Knight that in his personal affairs, as well as in all matters pertaining to the Quest, he will at all times conduct himself honorably and with courtesie and as a gentleperson - this principle prevailing even among the most dreadful of enemies (14).

6. The Legion of Ragnarok is an appendage of the Order of Yggdrasil dedicated, for the present, specifically to dealing with problems associated with personal insult or injury to members of the Order of Yggdrasil. In most instances this would pertain to slanderous media elements or anyone else treating any OY Knight unjustly. LR Knights are also empowered to self-initiate and act autonomously. The esoteric inner circle here is the Sentinels of Thor.

7. Founded Autumn Sabbat, September 22, 1985, on the southwest shore of Surry Lake in NH, a special corps of highly trained atavistic Berserkers are designated WLO Werewolves, also completely autonomous. Martial prowess here must include attainment of the higher belts in any effective hand to hand system, plus high proficiency with all commonly used weapons. This attainment must precede self-initiation.

8. Military rank will exactly parallel those of the armed forces in one's own country and will use the same insignias in the same positioning. Criteria for promotion and demotion will also be parallel. Rank is carried over from former service and is recognized herein. Both LR and Werewolves will follow same procedures as Army in this regard.

9. For all WLO Knights, also founded September 22, 1985, are Special Orders for Valor with appropriate decorations. These are arranged from highest to lowest on left pocket of uniform:

	Legion Ragnarok	Air Force	Navy	Army/Werewolves
Extreme Valor	Titans	Hypogriff	Sea Serpent	Dragon
Great Valor	Behemoth	Pegasus	Narwhal	Chimera
Invaluable Service	Bull	Eagle	Dolphin	Lion
Unusual Service	Star	Star	Star	Star

10. There will be signs for all branches of service in appropriate Tatva shapes and colors, to use only where insignia would be excessive or unduly extravagant. Standard international symbols will be used within the Tatva signs whenever possible.

11. The Oath of Knighthood should be read and contemplated first. Here the choice is made as to one's branch of military service. The Oath is performed as part of the Grand Ritual of Initiation ahead. Then with sword hand on the book "World Libertarian Revolution" and the other hand raised in a fist denoting Thor's Hammer, the candidate must declare his Allegiance to the Order. Dubbing with sword, dagger, or Athame is done with sword hand, first right, then left shoulder. LR or WW initiation will simply substitute appropriate designation here.

Footnotes:

12. This ritual with appropriate modifications will be used to found all other Orders within the TRS.

13. The ideal attitude if one survives, even in a World decimated, is illustrated by the author's projected reaction (June 19, 1983) to emerging from a fallout shelter after a nuclear war, knowing at least that most who caused the war are now dead, "And when the smoke has cleared, Sir Fenris will stand triumphant in the Sun, the pommel of his sword glistening. And from his lips will softly emerge the exultant adoration "This too is God."

14. Inspirational tokens such as scalps, ears, fingers, penises, or testicles should never be taken, even from those who practice such barbarities themselves. Remember the Golden Rule.

On the Purging of the West (15)

Ne~ 10 OYN

August 27, 1983
Ravenhurst
Royalston, Massachusetts

———

The citadels of human rottenness are often priceless architectural treasures which can be ritually cleansed and reconsecrated to higher purposes at some point in the future. Take heart!

"Beware the cowardly slaves of false and unnatural prophets. Cast them out and shun them, for they are the shamefast servants of vileness!"

"Eventually it will be proclaimed throughout the land that these false ones are false, and wherever they shall walk they shall walk ashamed, and in that time it will be clearly seen that they have been terribly terribly swollen, nay, bloated, with the wretched false importancy of the lower self, and that their words have been merely the vile banal trumpetings therefrom."

"We shall ride triumphantly through the streets in bright armor upon white horses, the corpses of the impotent weakling slaves of darkness lining the walkways at each side, their blood running out and filling the gutters at our feet!

Then shall begin their conversion into ash for our fields, and the recasting by fire of their holy chalices and idols, of gold under Sun, of silver under Moon, from icons of shame and meekness into gleaming images of Truth.

And we shall fashion their holy places into strongholds of pleasure and their skulls will adorn the rafters and gaze down upon us as we enjoy our naked women upon their holy altars."

Liber Heraldicae

Ne~ 8 OYN

February 2, 1983
Ravenhurst

Introduction

Flags for individual use should be fashioned from the descriptions here as individual circumstances permit. Recommended size is 32" x 40". These should be displayed on walls in meeting places, in one's private office or Place d' Arms. When this is problematical, they can simply be held strongly in mind:

Order at Peace in the North

Order at War in the East

Aethemera in the South

Nation in the West.

Armor is of course these days, purely ceremonial, but can be fashioned and worn for recreational jousting by horse masters possessing the means. For most it should be merely visualized and contemplated inspirationally, or could even be illustrated in paintings or drawings.

Dress uniforms should be attractive in style and cut, and are probably best based upon the rank-equivalent uniforms of one's own country. Such could be obtained from military surplus, then be bleached and dyed the appropriate color, or could be custom tailored locally. Field uniforms, at this stage, should only be worn at clandestine gatherings. Dress uniforms however, can be worn out and about town, especially on holidays. One can parry frivolous inquiry with the casual assertion that one is on the way to a costume ball, which is of course, a very good occasion to wear and enjoy them.

Insignia and Special Order pins of the required type can, strangely enough, usually best be procured from vendors at large agricultural fairs in summer or sometimes at novelty shops in cities. These should be small and tasteful, usually cloisonné and chosen with an eye to uniformity in size and style.

Traditional heraldic terminology is used and attributed thusly:

Gules - red - valor

Or - yellow (or gold)

Azure - blue - justice

Argent - white (silver w arms or armor) - purity

Sable – black

Note: Since the following flags correspond as indicated, it is suggested that these be displayed in different rooms to keep one flag per wall. For example - estate flag is most appropriate in dining hall.

Estate in the North

Legion of Ragnarok in the North

Family Coat of Arms in the East

Werewolves in the East

State or Province in the West.

Colors and Arms

I. Aethemera

In the tinctures here used, tribute is paid to the British Commonwealth of Nations, to France, and to the United States of America for many of the Libertarian ideals for which they have stood for in the past. The thirteen stars serve the dual function of special salute to the Founding Fathers of the Thirteen Colonies of the United States and of representing something which is higher than the twelve stars usually symbolizing government, namely, government limited to utmost degree. The Sun and Moon represent the Solar and Lunar principles. Aethemera is thus served "under Sun and Moon and Stars" astronomically, spiritually, and heraldically.

~ Flag: Ore border, deep azure field with thirteen argent stars surrounding central ten rayed ore Sun, argent crescent Moon in upper left of field with horns facing right.

II. Order of Yggdrasil at Peace (North)

~ Flag: Argent border, azure field, central argent World Tree Yggdrasil.

III. Order of Yggdrasil at War (East)

~ Flag: Ore border, deep azure field, central argent goat head with ore eyes, gules tips on ore horns, one pair perpendicular argent crossbones centered facing upright on either side of head.

~ Shield: Same as flag with extra pair of crossbones centered upright under head.

~ Armor: Argent, azure plume, argent goat's head visor.

~ Arms: Argent lance with gules tip, argent mace, sword and dagger of choice.

~ Horse: Best available, preferably white or at least with white extremities, azure blanket with argent border.

~ Personal Standard: Design of choice. This same on torso of armor.

~ Horse breast plate: Ore border, deep azure field, ore Aethemeran Sun.

IV. WLO Werewolves (16)

~ Flag: Ore border, gules field, central argent wolf head with ore eyes, one pair perpendicular argent crossbones centered facing upright on either side of head.

~ Shield: Same as flag with extra pair of crossbones centered upright under head.

~ Armor: Argent, gules plume, argent wolf's head visor.

~ Arms: Argent lance with gules tip, argent mace, sword and dagger of choice.

~ Horse: Best available, preferably white or at least with white extremities, gules blanket with ore border.

~ Personal Standard: Design of choice. This same on torso of armor.

~ Horse breast plate: Ore border, deep azure field, ore Aethemeran Sun.

V. Legion of Ragnarok

~ Flag: Argent border, sable field, central argent skull and crossbones facing straight ahead in traditional style with gules eyes connoting fire -

Thor's Jack O Lantern.

~ Shield: Same as flag.

~ Armor: Sable, gules plume, argent death's head visor.

~ Arms: Sable lance with gules tip, sable mace, sword and dagger of choice.

~ Horse: Best available, preferably black or at least with black extremities, sable blanket with argent border.

~ Horse breast plate: Argent border, gules field, ore Aethemeran Sun.

Liber Heraldicae

Part II

Ne~ 10 OYN

April 19, 1985
Winding Brook Lodge
Keene, New Hampshire

Dress Uniforms

Cap	Crest	Insignia	Collars	Right Pocket	Uniform	Trous Strp	Signs
		On Cap	Left-Right				
LR	Sun	Skl+Bns	LR-WLO	Yggdrasi	Black	Orange	Prithivi
Air Force	Sun	Griffin	OY-WLO	Yggdrasi	Sky Blue	Red	Vayu
Navy	Sun	Orca	OY-WLO	Yggdrasi	Sea Grn	Red	Apas
Army	Sun	Goat	OY-WLO	Yggdrasi	Tan	Red	Tejas
Werewolves	Sun	Wolf	WW-LO	Yggdrasi	Gray	Red	Tej

Field Uniforms

R Helmet	L Helmet	Cap	Collars	Right Pocket	Uniform
			Left-Right		
LR	Sun	Skl+Bns	LR-WLO	Skl+Bns	Black
WLO	Sun	Insignia	OY-WLO	Insignia	Camouflage
WW	Sun	Wolf	WW-WLO	Wolf	Camouflage

If the time comes when there are WLO Knights who are not also members of the OY, then collar designations will be WLO both left and right.

Footnotes:

15. Quotations are from Elof II. Last is from "Portent of Victory." From the standpoint of our goals the violent aspect of this should not be taken literally but merely contemplated with a Berserker's delight for the inspirational value.

16. Heraldic information on Werewolves and LR was added here later.

"Hail Aethemera!"

Magick Lamp above my head,
Shines as a beacon bright.
North - Yggdrasil is at my back,
East - Athame forged in Light.

Lamen hangs upon my chest,
Gandr - South - Fire is the test.
Sun rides high in azure sky,
Mead Horn in the West.

Our swords are honed for battle,
Loins girded with bright mail.
The Winds of Thor will guide our ships,
And fill our painted sails.

Ravens aloft, Wolves at my side,
I'll hue and flail and brand.
Berserker till the end of days,
Then rest my red right hand.

Diamond Stars will light the way,
Moon silver from afar.
Sun shine someday on golden shore,
Of bright Aethemera.

Winter 1988
Castle on the Green
Lyndonville, Vermont

"Ceremony for Founding Day" (17)

Ne~ 10 OYN

July 19, 1983
Ravenhurst
West Royalston, Massachusetts

———

0. Preliminary Preparations

I. Rejoicing in the Sun (18)

II. Assumption of Appropriate God Form (19)

Vibration of the Appropriate God Name

III. Tracing Pentagrams of White Flame to the Four Quarters (20)

IV. Blowing of Horn Once to Each of the Four Quarters

Salutation to Appropriate Deity (21)

V. Commemoration:

"The purpose of this most distinguished of all possible convocations is to commemorate, celebrate, and reaffirm the original purposes stated upon the great occasion of the founding of the mighty concept of Aethemera and of the Order of Yggdrasil - Liberty Triumphant and Eternal."

Drinking of the Mead of Inspiration

Reading of Liber Aethemerae

Reading of Liber Sangrealis

"In Furtherance of the New Aeon.

Love is the Law. Love Under Will.

Hail Yggdrasil!"

Commencement of Festivities

"Ritualis Grandis Initiatii"

Ne~ 4 OYN

July, 1980
Ravenhurst

---

0. Preliminaries

I. Rejoicing in the Sun

II. Assumption of Appropriate God Form

Vibration of Appropriate God Name

III. Tracing Pentagrams of White Flame to the Four Quarters

IV. Blowing of Horn to the Four Quarters

Salutation to Appropriate Diety

V. Drinking of the Mead of Inspiration

Oath of Knighthood

"I, (Name of Knight), in the Great Name of Yggdrasil, do pledge myself eternally to the principles of the Order of Yggdrasil and declare my wish that should I ever falter in my loyalty to the Quest, Liberty Triumphant and Eternal, that I hope my head to be severed from my body. By the strength and authority that I receive from the All One, I do proclaim myself

Sir (Name of Knight)

irrevocably in service to Our Lady Liberty-Aethemera, to whom I pledge my life and arms in unfailing vigilance under Sun and Moon and Stars to the end of days.

"In Furtherance of the New Aeon.

Love is the Law. Love Under Will.

Hail Yggdrasil!"

Commencement of Festivities

Footnotes:

17. Also is a general celebration of Liberty.

18. See "Transpersonal Psychology".

Author Grade Attainment

Hermetic Order of the Golden Dawn

	9 = 2
	8 = 3
	7 = 4
	6 = 5
	5 = 6
	4 = 7
	3 = 8
January 11, 1993	2 = 9
December 3, 1992	1 = 10
October 28, 1992	0 = 0

Ordo Templi Orientis

December 23, 1983	9
December 22, 1983	8
October 22, 1983	7
Autumn Sabbat 1983	6
Sep 11, 1983	5
Lughnasadh	4+1/2
June 25, 1983	4
June 11, 1983	3
April 26, 1983	2
March 18, 1983	1
February 25, 1983	0

OTO Notes

The premise of OTO activity is the utilization of "sex magick."
The first nine digress involve only heterosexual methodology.
Crowley later created two more degrees for those so inclined.

Approach OTO from standpoint of Libertarian Quest rather than
attainment of power, wear hooded black robe, and achieve neuronal
imprinting for each degree via deep concentration rather than orgasm.

The following journal entries chronicle the parts of designated rituals that
involve spontaneous individual response apart from official text:

Feb 25 At 12:00 PM finish 0 OTO
"My object in enrolling myself among you is to attain your allegiance in
defense of World Libertarian Revolution."
Saladin replies "So be it."
My sustenance and comfort, "Meditation upon my Quest."

June 11 c 8:15 PM Finish 3 OTO
P. 90 "...of our Order. I have regular charter on the Spirit Plane from the
Grandmaster Baphomet, as one who is continuing his work. I promise
always..."

June 25 At 3:53 PM finish 4 OTO Ritual
P. 115 During ritual, immediately after I say "...that I am" a young man
and red-haired woman approach...

Rosicrucian Order

December 29, 2013	10 = 1
	Interrupted Study
February 16, 1984	9 = 2
	Interrupted Study
May 21, 1980	8 = 3
April 29, 1980	Confessio
December 8, 1979	7 = 4
Date Not Recorned	6 = 5
Date Not Recorned	5 = 6
November 27, 1978	4 = 7
September 18, 1978	3 = 8
June 9, 1978	2 = 9
February 21, 1978	1 = 10
November 1, 1977	Atrium 3
June 25, 1977	Atrium 2
February 22, 1977	Atrium 1
Summer 1961	Initiol Inquiry

Order of the Ten Rayed Star

Destiny - 11 TRS - Council of Asgard after Ragnarok
Life's Highest Purposes

Yggdrasil	11	*White Wizard*	
Hel	10		
Mimir	9		
Odin	8		
Fenris	7		
Thor	6		
Tyr	5		
Balder	4		
Freya	3		
Kvasir	2		
Garm	1		
Frigga	0		
	Atrium 1	*Mt Baker Fnd CA*	

Rebirth - 10 TRS - Order of Yggdrasil in the East - Libertarian Revolution

	Yggdrasil	11	*Raven Friend*
	Hel	10	*Victory in Battle*
	Mimir	9	
	Odin	8	
	Fenris	7	
	Thor	6	
	Tyr	5	
	Balder	4	
Liberty Day 2015	Freya	3	Mt Lassen Founding OYE
Midsummer 1994	Kvasir	2	Consec Sword Wartooth
July 27 1993	Garm	1	Preperations at Elphinhaus
Autmn Sab1985	Frigga	0	Fnd SOV, WW Surry Lake NH
Summer 1953		Atrium 1	Learn Marksmanship

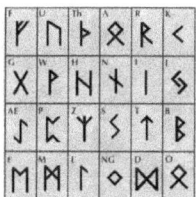

Mysticism - 9 TRS - Order of the Runemasters - Intuition and Wisdom

	Yggdrasil	11	*Runemaster*
	Hel	10	
	Mimir	9	
	Odin	8	
	Fenris	7	
	Thor	6	
	Tyr	5	
	Balder	4	
	Freya	3	
	Kvasir	2	
Yule Sabbat 2014	Garm	1	Stonehenge Fnd OR
January 26 1996	Frigga	0	Runes and Magickal Instruments
See Artis Magnae		Atrium 1	Early Divinations

Change - 8 TRS - World Libertarian Order - Worldwide Education

		Yggdrasil	11	*Gray Wizard*
		Hel	10	
		Mimir	9	
		Odin	8	*Constructive Societal Change*
		Fenris	7	
		Thor	6	
2013		Tyr	5	Publish with Amazon
June 2002		Balder	4	WCSF Invitation to Geneva
June 6 2001		Freya	3	Contact Media
March 5 2000		Kvasir	2	WLO Website
July 19 1998		Frigga	1	Finish Libertarian Writings
January 5 1996		Garm	0	Listing with EA
October 27 1983			Atrium 1	Liber Instructis

Disipline - 7 TRS - Order of the White Wolf - Special Achievement

		Yggdrasil	11	*Warrior of Light*
		Hel	10	
		Mimir	9	
		Odin	8	
		Fenris	7	
		Thor	6	
		Tyr	5	
		Balder	4	
		Freya	3	
		Kvasir	2	
2013		Garm	1	Excellent Reviews on Two Novels
2006 / 2010		Frigga	0	Phi Theta Capa CSN / Golden Key UNLX
April 27 1993			Atrium 3	End Alpine Gran Tour du Ski Sun Riv ME
Nov 13 1992			Atrium 2	End of Mountain Climbing Lost Lake NH
March 8 1983			Atrium 1	Lordship of Wolfhaven

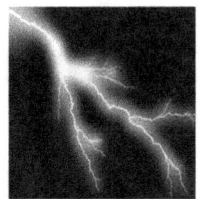

Beneficence - 6 TRS - Sentinels of Thor - Judicial Equalibrium

	Yggdrasil	11	*Ally of the Norns*
	Hel	10	
	Mimir	9	
	Odin	8	
	Fenris	7	
	Thor	6	
	Tyr	5	
	Balder	4	
	Freya	3	
Aut Sab 2014	Kvasir	2	*Glacier Park Founding ST*
May 21 2001	Garm	1	Write to Timothy McVeigh
April 22 1997	Frigga	0	Learn Judicial Equalibrium
August 24 1994		Atrium 2	Begin AMD Activity
Summer 1964		Atrium 1	Early Judicial Activity

Courage - 5 TRS - Legion of Ragnarok - Martial Prowess

	Yggdrasil	11	*Berserker*
	Hel	10	
	Mimir	9	
	Odin	8	
	Fenris	7	
	Thor	6	
	Tyr	5	*Attainment of Berserker Ideal*
	Balder	4	
	Freya	3	
Freyfaxi 2014	Kvasir	2	Mt Hood Founding LR
Dates Forgotten	Garm	1	Victories (1)
Summer 1963	Frigga	0	Chivalry Supersedes Violence
Winter 1960		Atrium 3	Hand to Hand Victory as Warrior
Summer 1959		Atrium 2	First Martial Study
Spring 1953		Atrium 1	Use of Intelligence to Avoid Violence

Power - 4 TRS - Order of Suna - Integrated Higher Self

	Yggdrasil	11	*Dragonmaster*
	Hel	10	
	Mimir	9	
	Odin	8	
	Fenris	7	
	Thor	6	
	Tyr	5	
	Balder	4	
	Freya	3	
	Kvasir	2	
Midsum 2014	Garm	1	Great Salt Lake Founding OS
August 5 1995	Frigga	0	Oath of Silence
April 12 1987		Atrium 2	Save life of Paula (Katy)
Spring 1972		Atrium 1	Save Lives Barbara, Sergio

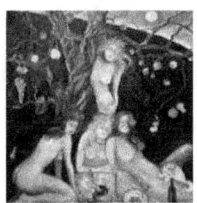

Enjoyment - 3 TRS - Coven of the Witches (2) - Sex and Romance

	Yggdrasil	11	Witch Friend
	Hel	10	
	Mimir	9	
	Odin	8	
	Fenris	7	
	Thor	6	
	Tyr	5	
	Baldur	4	
	Freya	3	
	Kvasir	2	
	Garm	1	
	Frigga	0	
January 30 2910		Atrium 5	Consummation of Oath made 1985
Mayday 2003		Atrium 4	MGM Dome Founding CW
Samhain 1980		Atrium 3	Dionysius f Zabeth's Coven Salem
October 30 1977		Atrium 2	HBTT Working (3)
August 1953		Atrium 1	Priapic Celeb w Debbie Chandler

Magick - 2 TRS - Children of Odin - Archetypal Magick

	Yggdrasil	11	*Norse Magician*
	Hel	10	
	Mimir	9	
	Odin	8	
	Fenris	7	
	Thor	6	
April 14 2001	Tyr	5	CO Website
Yule 1996	Balder	4	Sabbat Celeb Mythology of the North
Feb 2 1995	Freya	3	Begin CFA Activity
March 19 1994	Kvasir	2	Consecration Odin Dagger
Spring Sab1993	Garm	1	Fnd CO, OWW, CFA Echo Lake (4)
August 11 1988	Frigga	0	Fin Bavarian Castle Room
Oct 15 1978		Atrium 2	Init Gesith Seax Wicca
Summer 1953		Atrium 1	First Critical Thinking

Energy - 1 TRS - Order of Yggdrasil in the North - Spiritual Energizing

February 9 1988	Yggdrasil	11	Seeker of Thule. WWII History
February 12 1983	Hel	10	Fnd OYN, WLO Burial Hill MA
June 20 1983	Mimir	9	Sigil of Irols
January 23 1983	Odin	8	Knighthood World Libertarian Order
November 9 1982	Fenris	7	Consecration Ten Rayed Star
August 25 1981	Thor	6	Esbat Ars Magna, Three Scrolls (5)
June 1981	Tyr	5	Evolutionary Dualism (6)
March 5 1979	Balder	4	K+C of HGA Tully Mountain
Imbolic 1979	Freya	3	Formal Adoption of Chivalry
October 15 1978	Kvasir	2	Consecration of Star Hunter (7)
Midsum 1977	Garm	1	Begin Charging Elixir
Samhain 1975	Frigga	0	First Formal Magickal Ritual (8)
Summer 1957		Atrium 1	Occasional Flame Ritual

Stability - 0 TRS - Order of Midgard - Ongoing Plans

	Yggdrasil	11	Oathmaker - Life After Ragnarok
	Hel	10	Founding of TRS
	Mimir	9	Mastery of the Runes
Jul 1998	Odin	8	Continue Libertarian Writings
September 2006	Fenris	7	General Study
Apr 1997	Thor	6	Judicial Equalibrium
	Tyr	5	Martial Study
	Balder	4	Forest Hikes
Nov 1974	Freya	3	Appreciation of Witches
	Kvasir	2	Preparation for Ragnarok
Apr 1997	Garm	1	Coninue in Good Health
Mar 2001	Frigga	0	Allegiance of Fafnir
Plow Chrmng 1997		Atrium 3	Sabbat Fnd OM Pyramid Lake NV
See Artis Magnae		Atrium 2	Early Efforts (9)
See Adven EFM		Atrium 1	Prim Ed, Cub Scouts, Sec Ed

Preliminary Attainment

December 23 1995	First Asatru Ritual
Beltane 1983	Master of Magical Arts Degree
April 6 1983	Construction of Upper Ravenshenge
March 17 1983	9th Ordo Sangrealis Baphometis
February 2 1983	Writing of Sangrealis and Dagsljus
November 8 1982	Writing of "Convocati"
May 1982	Construction of Lower Ravenshenge
October 27 1980	Beginning of Scroll T
October 4 1980	Beginning of Scroll E
July 1980	Conception of Ritualis Grandis Propositi
1979	Writing of Ritualis Dotum Animi
February 1978	Beginning of Scroll A
October 29 1976	Photographs as Magician
Fall 1955	Magickal Diorama

Footnotes:

1. Include here four "out on the town late at night" victories, all of which saved the author's life.

2. Modern EvD Coven ideally has fourteen members. Fourteenth herein is of course, the author.

3. The Three Witches involved, plus Gretchen VanRoon are, of course, committed elsewhere, but in this context actually represent a small coven (harem) in the truest sense.

4. Followed on June 17 by a special introduction of the CO to other Nordic groups.

5. Celebrates "finish" of the Three Scrolls on August 16. This material now comprises Lion's share of the book "Traditional Arcane Teachings".

6. Aided by understanding international finance. OYN is concerned in some measure with Evolutionary Dualist (EvD) goals. For bigger dose see "New World Order: Just Say No!"

7. War Dagger, Liberator, replaces this as OYN Athame in new consecration Lughnasadh 1992.

8. Initial format from Anton Szandor LaVey. Soon after, increase archetypal inspirations to include celestial pantheons with infernal. Why settle for less? By way of streamlining, later go to purely Nordic archetypes in keeping with family heritage. Unfortunately, only surviving photographs are of earliest ritual chamber.

9. Includes all activities relating to the Five Elemental Goals not mentioned herein, from creation of vitamin program to guitar playing. Mostly of little significance, except to author.

Implements

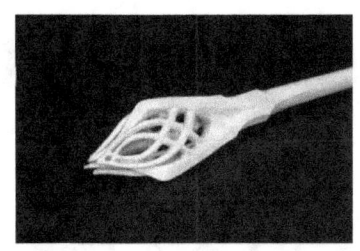

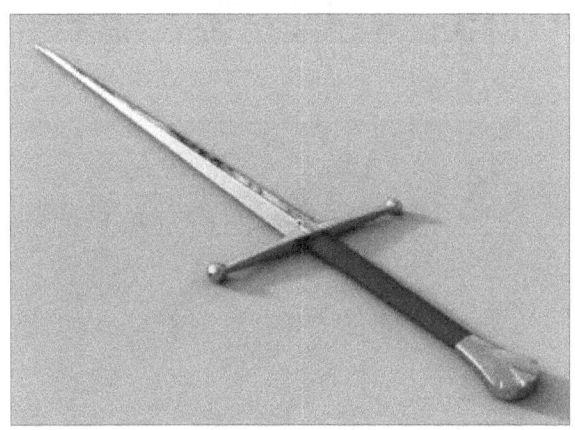

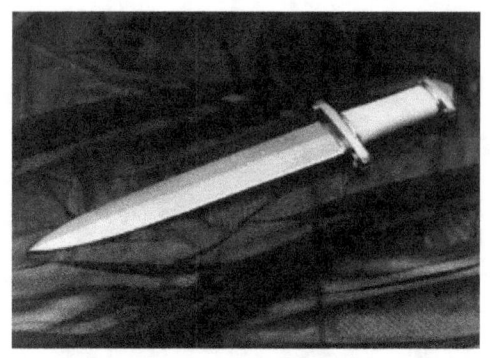

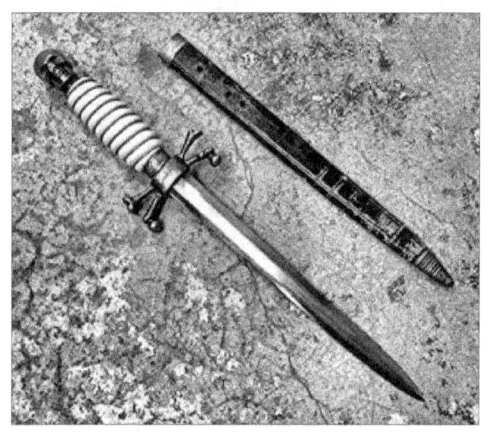

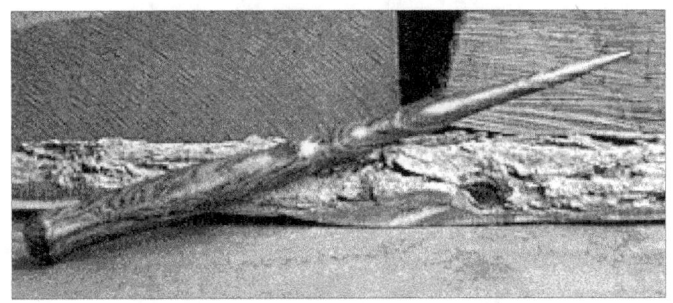

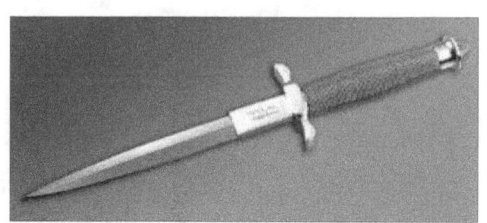

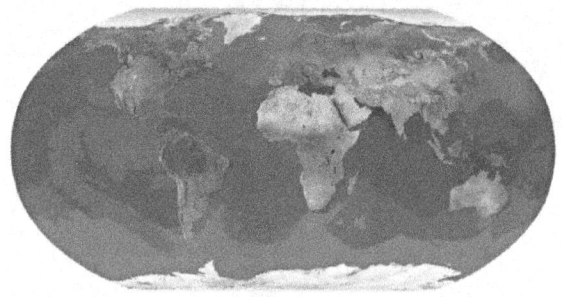

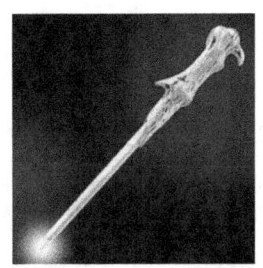

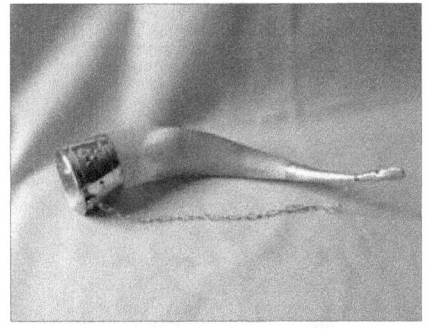

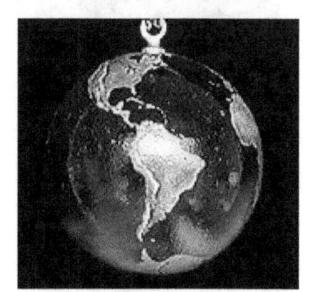

Liber Historiae Occasi

BC:	c. 10,000	Destruction of Atlantis
	c. 3,100	Hermes helps build pyramids. Writes Book of the Dead
	-----	Hermes engraves the Emerald Tablet
	-----	Hermes authors the Scroll of Thoth
	-----	Odin discovers the Runes
	2,350	Enoch views Emerald Tablets with the Angel Metatron
	1,800	Abraham's wife finds Emerald Tablet of Hermes
	1,250	Moses appears to destroy Emerald Tablets from Metatron
	1,060	Witch of Endor aids Saul raising the Prophel Samuel
	950	Solomon builds Temple, recasts pommel of Grail Sword
	753	Romulus founds Rome
	638	Birth of Zoroaster
	580	Birth of Pythagoras
	330	Alexander finds Emerald Tablet of Hermes
	0	Birth of Jesus bar Joseph
AD:	-----	Fall of Rome, Rise of Gnosticism
	216	Birth of Mani
	1000	Icelandic Assembly chooses Christianity
	1244	Surrender of Citadel at Montsegur
	1291	Founding of Switzerland
	1300	Moses De Leon reveals Zohar
March 18	1314	Murder of Jacques de Molay and Templars
	1329	Tarot appears in Germany
	-----	Beginning of decline in worldly power for Inquisition
	1581	John Dee and Edward Kelly receive Enochian Tablets
July 4	1776	Founding of the United States of America
	1875	Birth of Aleister Crowley
	1913	Fall of United States to international banking interests
	1915	Rebirth of the Rosicrucian Order in the United States
	1918	Treaty of Versailles for future financing of WW II
	1939	Britain declares war on Germany
March	1944	Germans discover Pagan Grail at Montsegur
	1965	Tolkien publishes "Lord of the Rings"
Beltane	1966	Anton Zandor Lavey founds Church of Satan
	1969	Founding of Libertarian Party in the United States
	1972	Founding of the Asatru Alliance in the United States
	1989	Fall of Communism in Europe

Footnote:

1. Not to be confused with other orders of the same name.

Books Promoting Liberty Free Online

Non-Fiction

None Dare Call It Conspiracy by Gary Allen
Riveting inside history of globalist bankers right from the
beginning. More compelling than the best of novels. Only
chumps, jokers, and sleepwalkers have not read this yet.

The Occult Technology of Power by Robert Eringer
Explanation of how the Shadow Government rules, written
as though by one of the globalist bankers to be read
posthumously by his son as instruction on how to wield his
newly inherited power.

Our Nordic Race by Richard Kelly Hoskins
Explains who the Nordic peoples are, how their civilizations
have been destroyed in the past, and urges future
preservation of the Nordic race and culture.

Why Civilizations Self Destruct by Elmer Pendell
Scholarly history of the way in which earlier societies fell into
decay as the entire world is doing now.

The Fulfillment of Evolutionary Destiny by Eric F. Magnuson
Explains how we can defeat globalist totalitarian socialism
with a far more workable worldwide Libertarian Free
Enterprise system.

Holocaust: 120 Questions and Answers
by Charles E. Weber
From the Institute for Historical Review. One of many
interesting contra-orthodox volumes refuting standard
wartime disinformation.

Fiction

Hunter by Andrew MacDonald
Engrossing novel explains how to kill the everyday public enemies of your country covertly as a heroic citizen.

New World Order: The Final Solution by Roy C. Peterson
Exciting novel explains how to exterminate the growing legions of sub humanity in massive numbers privately, but also how to legally establish world liberty, prosperity, and peace without killing anybody.

Eric F. Magnuson Short Biography

Eric Fenris Magnuson was born in Massachusetts. His parents were corporate business people. At Northeastern University, he studied science and English. Supporting himself as an antique dealer, he amassed a library of over four thousand books and began a diverse program of private study. Moved by the need to create something that would outlive him, on February 12, 1983 he founded an activist organization, the World Libertarian Order. After a six year tour du ski. he moved to Lake Wildwood California, and at present continues his writings in Montreal, Quebec.

Fimbul Winter Books

Writings of Eric F Magnuson

Balanced Healthy Living / Absolute Individual Liberty /
Viable Evolutionary Spirituality

As director of the World Libertarian Order, I have worked for
peace and prosperity since the early 1980s. Most people
prefer fantasy to reality. Since my books deal only with
uncompromised truth, they are for the few, not the many.
I offer these writings for whatever good they may ultimately
accomplish in the world. They are all good quality glossy
paperbacks at a low price. To see them, visit your favorite
book vendor (e.g. Amazon, Barnes + Noble) and search
"Eric F Magnuson " under Books. You fill find independent
reviews and author descriptions.

~ Eric Fenris Magnuson ~

Evolution Family Reader
Eric F. Magnuson

Evolutionary Psychology
Eric F. Magnuson

World Libertarian Revolution
Eric F. Magnuson

New World Order
Just Say No!
Eric F. Magnuson

Traditional Arcane Exemplars
Eric F. Magnuson

Mythology of the North
Eric F. Magnuson

Arcane Fraternal Orders
Eric F. Magnuson

Magickal Pictures
Eric F. Magnuson

The
Adventures
of
Eric F. Magnuson

Book I

The Life of an American Libertarian Writer

The
Adventures
of
Eric F. Magnuson

Book II

The Life of an American Libertarian Writer

End the Subverted Media Monopoly

Stop the Parasites

It is important to view these books and videos, because globalists control the mass media. They slant the news to destroy ethnic and cultural identity, so that host populations will accept one world government, giving their banker associates absolute financial monopoly. They do not use logical persuasion, but in a matter-of-fact way, suggest that the majority of people already believe in their goals. This is to make us feel that we will be out of step with current trends, and be disliked for not embracing the same viewpoints.

The subconscious mind is pre-lingual and cannot be influenced by words. Whenever possible, the media masters program us with pictures designed to elicit primal emotions. Even if we find out the truth from statistics later, the subconscious will still believe in the pictures.

We must rid ourselves of these hell-rotters once and for all. We cannot learn about superior alternatives to globalization until there are laws to protect societies against media monopoly. The fairest way is to require that the percentage of media ownership by any special interest group not exceed the percentage of that group in the national population. Who, but monopolists, would object to this? Read how things stand now, then ask yourself why any of this is tolerated:

Non-Fiction

New World Order: Seek and Destroy
from Viking Media Favorites
This compilation from many sources explains all you will
ever need to know to maximize your resistance to predatory
globalization.

None Dare Call It Conspiracy by Gary Allen
Riveting inside history of globalist bankers right from the
beginning. More compelling than the best of novels. Only
chumps, jokers, and sleepwalkers have not read this
one yet.

The Occult Technology of Power by Robert Eringer
Explanation of how the Shadow Government rules, written
as though by one of the globalist bankers to be
read posthumously by his son as instruction on how to wield
his newly inherited power.

Our Nordic Race by Richard Kelly Hoskins
Explains who the Nordic peoples are, how their civilizations
have been destroyed in the past, and urges future
preservation of the Nordic race and culture.

Why Civilizations Self Destruct by Elmer Pendell
Scholarly history of the way in which earlier societies fell into
decay as the entire world is doing now.

The Fulfillment of Evolutionary Destiny by Eric F. Magnuson
Explains how we can defeat globalist totalitarian socialism
with a far more workable worldwide Libertarian Free
Enterprise system.

Revolution: And How to Do It in a Modern Society
by Professor Kai Murros
Things are happening in Europe that should be happening elsewhere.

Holocaust: 120 Questions and Answers
by Charles E. Weber
From the Institute for Historical Review. One of many interesting contra-orthodox volumes refuting standard wartime disinformation.

Fiction

Hunter by Andrew MacDonald
This engrossing novel explains the truth about many world problems, including how to kill the everyday public enemies of your country covertly as a heroic citizen.

New World Order: The Final Solution by Roy C. Peterson
Exciting novel explains how to exterminate the growing legions of sub-humanity in massive numbers privately, but also how to legally establish world liberty, prosperity, and peace without killing anybody.